AID POLICY IN WAR-TORN COUNTRIES

*Promoting Development
in Conflict Situations:
The Case of Angola*

GW00634049

Mafalda ~~Duarte~~

University Press of America,® Inc.
Dallas · Lanham · Boulder · New York · Oxford

Copyright © 2003 by
University Press of America,® Inc.
4501 Forbes Boulevard
Suite 200
Lanham, Maryland 20706
UPA Acquisitions Department (301) 459-3366

PO Box 317
Oxford
OX2 9RU, UK

Library of Congress Cataloging-in-Publication Data

Duarte, Mafalda.
Aid policy in war-torn countries : promoting development in
conflict situations : the case of Angola / Mafalda Duarte.
p.   cm
Includes bibliographical references.
1. Economic assistance—Angola. 2. United Nations—Economic
assistance. 3. Angola—Economic conditions. 4. War—Economic
aspects—Angola. I. Title.

HC950 .D834 2002
338.91'09673—dc21   2002032043 CIP

ISBN 0-7618-2409-X (paperback : alk. ppr.)

This research is dedicated with love
to the memory of my grandmother,
Maria da Conceição Madeira

TABLE OF CONTENTS

PART I

THE THEORETICAL BACKGROUND

PART II
THE CASE STUDY

APPENDIX

LIST OF TABLES AND GRAPHICS

APPENDIX

ACKNOWLEDGMENTS

Firstly, I would like to thank my dissertation supervisor, Frances Cleaver, for supporting the whole project of the research since the beginning and for all the guidance given throughout its progress. Secondly, I want to mention my sponsor, Ministério da Ciência e Tecnologia (PRAXIS XXI—Portugal) and the European Union for the financial support. Without the scholarship granted it would have been impossible to pursue this research. Moreover, I want to express my gratitude to all the people in Angola who helped me in establishing the necessary contacts for the interviews and all the interviewed people for being willing to contribute to the research.

As this represents the final stage of the Master's Degree, I want to thank my parents, Maria de Lurdes and Victor Duarte and my brother, Nuno Duarte for the vital continuous support given to all the projects I conceive of doing. The last person I want to thank is Paulo Neto for being who he is.

PART I

THE THEORETICAL BACKGROUND

CHAPTER 1

INTRODUCTION

The dynamics in the international system have led to the shift, in terms of aid policy, from just relief assistance toward attempts to support development in emergency situations. The research carried out deals, precisely, with the dilemma of whether development can be pursued in conflict situations and how it can and should be done. This was the research subject chosen, firstly, because it seemed quite interesting to analyze an area which appears to be so paradoxical. Secondly, as we were unable to find case studies which would reflect people's opinion about this subject we decided to move forward and interview people from a war torn developing country society on this matter. Moreover, the importance of this research lies in the fact that if development interventions in war torn societies could be successful, the amount of aid going to relief assistance could be reduced and directed toward combating the causes of conflicts as well as the grounding of future development. We further believe that war-torn societies' population beliefs and their knowledge of what should be done in such cases is a very important step toward a better understanding of this dilemma. Additionally, the relevance of their opinion rests on the fact that they would be the 'instruments' and 'beneficiaries' of an improvement of development cooperation in war-torn countries.

In order to do this we will divide the research in two parts. On the first, theoretical part, we will identify the main dynamics of the new international system that led to the referred shift in terms of the aid paradigm. Secondly, we will present some arguments proposed by different studies supporting the new form of understanding aid in war-torn countries. Moreover, we will mention some of the measures, in terms of development cooperation, brought forward by these studies to be implemented in conflict situations.

On the second part, dealing with the results of the case study, we will bring up the results in terms of our main question, namely, whether people from a war-torn country believe in the possibility of pursuing development in such circumstances. Secondly, we will bring forward people's opinion about the measures referred on the first part of the study. Finally, in the conclusion the main ideas will be summarized.

Before starting the next section we would like to, already, ask for a conceptual clarification. From the study done we see the need to establish clear concepts and clear distinctions between humanitarian assistance, relief, emergency assistance, rehabilitation and development. The fact that each author makes his or her own interpretation of the concepts just adds to the already difficult task of establishing and distinguishing fields of work and responsibilities. In this study, we will use the concepts giving them the following meanings: emergency assistance will relate to relief, rehabilitation and development interventions;[1] humanitarian and relief assistance will be both relating to short-term supply of urgent inputs after emergency situations have occurred; rehabilitation will

---

1. In relation to emergencies we adopted the classification proposed by Buchanan-Smith and Maxwell (1994) of rapid onset, slow onset, 'permanent' and complex political emergencies. Rapid onset emergencies—earthquakes or floods; slow onset emergencies—those triggered by natural disasters such as droughts; 'permanent' emergencies—characterised by widespread structural poverty; and complex political emergencies—associated with conflict. In this research we will be referring to emergencies as complex political emergencies.

concern interventions between relief and development in emergency contexts;[2] and development interventions will be those long-term, evolutionary interventions which try to promote self-sufficiency on the part of the communities and governments.

---

2. However, this does not represent a chronological sequence and in fact one of the objectives of the study is precisely to question it.

CHAPTER 2

THE NEW INTERNATIONAL SYSTEM

In this section we will outline the main characteristics of the international system that helps us understand the shift, in terms of aid policy, from just supporting relief assistance toward attempts to support development in complex political emergencies in developing countries. Briefly, this shift appears to be the result of a narrowing of focus of international agendas in the North as well as of a merging of security and development concerns. A uniform way of understanding the relations within the states and the fact that security issues have been identified with development concerns caused development aid to be regarded as the foundation of stability. In this section, we will mainly rely on the analyses of Mark Duffield as we consider them the most relevant for our analysis.

In this context, the demise of political world movements that represented an alternative to the western liberal-democratic model of development was particularly important. At the same time that it encouraged widespread social and political change, the absence of a credible opposition to liberal democracy has also allowed a certain narrowing of international agendas in the North. Along with that process, aid policy appears to have narrowed as well. Having one dominant political model, it is perhaps understandable that the relations within the states should be viewed in an increasingly uniform light (Duffield, 1998).

Within this narrowing process, what is particularly interesting is the merging of security and development concerns. Aid policy has always played a political role. During the Cold War, security was basically conceived in terms of antagonism between states, military deterrence and the formation of political alliances and blocs.

It was to maintain these alliances that aid was frequently employed. Furthermore, relief and development were often seen as mutually exclusive under such conditions. The aid deployed was mostly related to relief objectives as development aid was considered to confer political legitimacy (Duffield, 1998). In this context, all geographical areas were relevant to maintain the ideological hegemony.

The demise of alternative political systems and the increasing focus on intra-state relations, however, led to a shift in the meaning of security and aid's relation to it. Rather than inter-state tensions, security objectives, are, now, more related to the regional implications for stability of internal matters such as poverty, crime, population growth or migration. Insofar as current approaches to development cooperation also intend to tackle these issues, there has been a merging of security and development concerns (Duffield, 1998). In this context, areas which can represent a direct source of instability to developed countries, as well as areas where key interests are in place, will be the areas where intervention will be privileged. This merging of security and development is quite relevant as it causes development to be regarded as the foundation of stability. Relief assistance is no longer sufficient and should not contradict or undermine the longer-term aims of development. Such changes underpin the shift, in terms of aid policy, from just relief assistance, toward attempts to support development in emergency situations. Many conflict resolution agencies, for example, attempt to go beyond the limitations of humanitarian aid by trying to address the causes of conflict directly. In dismissing the mutually exclusive nature of relief and development in emergency situations, such thinking has, however, contributed as well to a blurring of these categories.

Firstly, one example has been the creation of a form of 'development relief' in which the focus of assistance shifted from supporting people to that of strengthening institutions and processes (Duffield, 1998). Secondly, development has been, increasingly, reduced to relief. Rather than regarding these two as separate practices, the post-Cold War paradigm holds that relief should be provided in a way to foster people-centered development and humanitarian assistance has become the West's favored response to political crisis beyond its borders. In many aspects, this seems to be a projection of the way in which the West is attempting to solve its own problems. Both internally and in terms of relations with developing countries, the focus of Western countries public policy has shifted from attempting to manage growth and redistribution to trying to contain the effects of poverty and social exclusion (Duffield, 1997). Western countries seem to forget that, despite how valuable relief assistance has been in relieving immediate suffering, and how valuable it is to ask for a better relief assistance,[1] this kind of aid has made little impact on the underlying problems and causes of conflict. Given the new belief in fostering people centered development and giving the increasing levels of damage and social disruption, there seems to be a need for the revitalization of development goals. As Mark Duffield (1997, p. 530) mentions *'Given the decline in overall development funding and the high levels of damage and social disruption in conflict-affected areas, continuum thinking makes little sense without a revitalization of development goals.'*

Additionally, a new phenomenon also contributed to the increase in the amount of relief assistance delivered under war conditions.

---

1. One example of this better relief is the already mentioned 'development relief'—supporting people to strengthen institutions and processes. As it is mentioned in United Nations Development Programme (UNDP) (1994), if conceptualised, planned and implemented in isolation relief will replace development and breed long-term dependencies, undermine indigenous coping strategies and increase vulnerabilities.

Over the last decades there has been a move away from an international refugee regime focused almost exclusively on the obligations of receiving states. Increasingly, no country wants to accept refugees. This has prompted attempts to prevent large scale population movements crossing international boundaries through humanitarian assistance to support war-affected populations within their home countries. In less than a decade attempts to assist such populations entirely transformed the nature of humanitarian assistance. Mostly through a series of *ad hoc* Security Council resolutions, a key change had been the ability to provide relief assistance under war conditions. On the other hand, until the end of the 1980s warring parties usually denied humanitarian assistance to areas controlled by the opponents, largely as a result of the importance previously attached to dominant notions of non-interference in internal matters, a right still granted by Chapter 1 of the United Nations Charter. During the Cold War, United Nations (UN) interventions, for example, despite uncommon, took place on the basis of agreed cease-fire or clear peacekeeping agreements. Within the post-Cold War paradigm, however, negotiated access has become the principal means of expanding humanitarian assistance in internal wars (Duffield, 1997). Moreover, the instrument has become more and more sophisticated.[2]

Due to the already analyzed, post Cold War new understanding of security and development, these new operational tools can represent ways in which broadening development interventions in war conditions can become a possibility.

In conclusion, we can say that the dynamics in the international system have brought some important changes.

The merging of security and development means that the 'low politics' of poverty and human rights is increasingly becoming the 'high politics' of governments. As a result, there was the recogni-

---

2. It is increasingly common for UN integrated programs and even non-governmental organizations (NGOs), for example, to employ ex-military personnel as security advisors (Duffield, 1997).

tion of the necessity for considering the role of development in conflict situations. In addition, the increasing interest in humanitarian assistance originated new operational tools that have increased the scope of intervention in war affected countries. All these facts mean that there is a wide scope for improvement of development interventions.

What we will present, in the next section, are, precisely, some of the arguments in favor of the practical application of this new understanding of aid policy interventions in war-torn societies, as well as measures, in terms of development cooperation, proposed for those countries.

CHAPTER 3

RECENT FINDINGS ON AID POLICY

In this analysis we will mention the main arguments presented in recent studies justifying the promotion of development interventions in war-torn societies. Moreover, we will point out some of the principal measures that were proposed on those same studies in order for development interventions to be effective under complex political emergencies. We will, further, try to do it in an integrated way dividing the analysis in three groups. The first one concerns arguments and measures brought up by studies dealing with aid policy analyses. The second group relates to discussions and measures pointed out in studies analyzing conflict situations. Finally, the third group involves measures coming out of main ideas in development cooperation.

Aid Policy Analyses

As far as studies dealing with aid policy analyses are concerned, we will look at the 1998 World Bank Policy Research Report and its conclusions in terms of development cooperation for sound management countries and high distorted environments.[1]

---

1. High distorted countries are, according to the World Bank Policy Research Report (1998), those which don't have sound management. Sound management is defined on the basis of an index of economic policy (inflation, the budget surplus and trade openness) and a measure of

One of the main conclusions of the Report is that financial assistance leads to faster growth, poverty reduction and gains in social indicators in low-income countries with sound management (2.7 percent per capita compared with 0.5 percent per capita in high distorted environments).

In good management environments 1 percent of GDP in assistance translates to a sustained increase in growth of 0.5 percent points of GDP, to a reduction of poverty by 1 percent and an increase of 1.9 percent of GDP in private investment. According to the World Bank, low aid countries with sound management have grown at 2.2 percent per capita while the high aid group grew at 3.7 percent per capita. Furthermore, in countries with sound management aid projects were 86 percent successful whereas in countries with weak management the corresponding figure is 48 percent. The point is that *'(...) poor countries with good policies should receive more financing than equally poor countries with weak economic management.'* (World Bank, 1998, p.4). Secondly, improvements in economic institutions and policies in the developing world seem to be the key to a significant poverty reduction. Further reform in governance and policies would take 60 million people a year out of poverty. In countries with sound management, aid also seems to 'crowd in' private investment by a ratio of almost $2 to every $1 of aid. In these countries, aid increases the confidence of the private sector and supports important public services. In highly distorted environments, aid 'crowds out' private investment. In a poor management country 1 percent of GDP in aid is estimated to reduce private investment by 0.5 percent of GDP. The fourth conclusion relates to the value of development projects. According to the Report, the main objective of development

---

institutional quality which involves an assessment of the strength of the rule of law, the quality of public bureaucracy and the pervasiveness of corruption. We considered, in this analysis, war torn countries to be high distorted countries. Therefore, the measures the World Bank advises for those countries were considered for the case study.

projects should be to strengthen institutions and policies so that services can be effectively delivered. The most critical contribution of projects is not to increase funding for particular sectors, but to help improve service delivery by strengthening sectoral and local institutions. Fifthly, the best aid projects seem to be those which support civil society. The idea that many projects have supported in recent years—a participatory approach to service delivery—often resulted in impressive improvements.

Despite these conclusions, the World Bank Report assessed that aid can also nurture reform even in the most distorted environments. The case is to rely on other instruments to support development, requiring a 'focus on ideas and not money.' In many of these countries, the government is not providing effective policies or services, which is why government-to-government transfers have produced poor results. However, there are often champions of local or sectoral reform and aid at times has been effective supporting these initiatives. This work is staff-intensive and results in little disbursement of funds. Successful assistance here aims to help reformers develop and test their ideas. It aims to support knowledge creation in the sense of financing and evaluating innovations. Reformers usually have a long-term vision and they often need to develop the details of reform through innovation and evaluation. For reform to take place it requires a demonstration that it actually works. In this context, development projects can be a testing ground for ideas or concepts that are new to a country, demonstrating to the government and citizens what does and does not work.[2] This was the first measure (measure a) we proposed in the questionnaires and the results are discussed in the case study

---

2. Examples: contracting out public services, using NGOs or involving user groups in management. Two main benefits can be identified. One is the opportunity to devote resources to careful evaluation of experience. This kind of knowledge is an international public good and no government has sufficient incentive to evaluate or disseminate it. Secondly, donor projects can also help break the mentality that locks the public sector into ineffective arrangements (World Bank, 1998).

section. The second measure relates to the importance, as seen previously, of engaging civil society in the provision of services. According to the World Bank Report, effective aid should involve supporting civil society either to pressure the government to change or to take service provision directly into its own hands. This is measure b) in the case study.

In conclusion, assistance in high distorted environments should involve intensive staff input and small disbursements of money. *'The role of aid in difficult environments is to educate the next generation of leaders, disseminate information about policy and stimulate public debate where possible.'* (World Bank, 1998, p.48).[3] It is unfortunate, however, as the Report itself recognizes, to note that donors' ability to work in these environments has been hampered by an 'approval and disbursement culture' that does not value small-scale, staff-intensive activities.

Conflict Situation Analyses

We will now turn our attention to the second kind of studies dealing with discussions and measures pointed out in conflict situations analyses. All of them accept that conflict is one main reason for the underdevelopment of the countries which face them. In the specific case of Sub-Saharan Africa violent conflict is clearly assumed to be one main reason why 250 million people—half of the region's population—lived below the poverty line in the mid-1990s (Colleta and Nezam, 1998). However, let's, briefly, analyze what have been the main causes behind the recurrence of violent conflicts. Most wars seem to be fought in countries which are poor, divided by identity and gross disparities in wealth and which have lacked the political and legal systems

---

3. Once more, we would like to remark that the World Bank didn't mention the implementation of these ideas in war-torn countries. In the case study section we will analyze whether the interviewed people from Angola believe in its implementation or not in their country.

necessary to manage change without recourse to violence. Inequality and unfair competition for land to live on or farm, jobs, access to water or minerals to exploit, have been at the root of many wars, particularly when these conditions are intensified through external shocks or economic austerity programs.

Moreover, it seems that conflicts are not so much about the lack of resources *per se*, as injustice: social, economic, and political structures which maintain the dominance of an in-group at the center of power, over an out-group at the periphery, most of the times lacking the basic rights. Ethnic tensions have, thus, increased, as people feel that they suffer because of belonging to their group and blame others for this. Furthermore, where states are too corrupt, undemocratic, or have collapsed and do not have an independent judiciary to punish those guilty of economic and social grievance and gross abuses of human rights, violent change is likely to occur. In addition, where the state is unable to provide basic security or to satisfy fundamental social and welfare needs, loyalties can shift to radical groups or warlords intending to fuel conflicts (Agerbak, 1991).

As we can see, all these causes are mainly related to the absence of an effective and accountable government. Apart from the measures seen previously in the World Bank Report, we will analyze different measures related to the causes of conflicts and effectiveness of donor interventions. To note, nevertheless, that the main causes of conflicts are related to developmental factors and in this sense it is understandable that the measures should mainly reflect development concerns.

Bakwesegha (1998), for example, emphasizes the weakness of democracy as an important cause of conflicts. According to the author, the unfamiliarity of democracy, especially in the African continent, makes many people take democracy for elections, being unable to acknowledge that democracy is a process of building institutions which are democratic, economically self-reinforcing and self-sustaining and which are capable of absorbing instability.

Therefore, as the best custodians of the democratic transition and implementation in any country are the nationals themselves, he refs the importance of teaching people the meaning of democratic institutions, how to defend them and how to use them as tools for absorbing conflicts. This is measure c) in our case study.[4]

The weakness of civil society and social capital[5] has, also, been pointed out, as seen previously, as a factor contributing to the underdevelopment as well as to conflicts in developing societies. In order to reinforce civil society, Scharf (1998), mentioned that, over the long-term, donors could support institutions such as citizens' advice bureau and local media (among other institutions that we decided not to include in our analysis). He brought up the measure while analyzing the building blocks for peace building and reconciliation but we decided to take the idea and investigate about its application in a war-torn society. This is measure d) in our case study.

The third measure on this group was brought forward by Colleta and Nezam (1998). When analyzing the World Bank's experience with conflict, they mentioned the following measure for conflict-ridden situations. Namely, the need to develop an understanding of the context, dynamics and assistance needs, in order to design appropriate interventions when conditions permit (measure e) in the case study).

The OECD/DAC (1999) Report, when analyzing the external assistance in conflict situations, also defines some measures from which we decided to use one in our primary research.

---

4. This measure was not proposed to be implemented in a war-torn country. However, we decided to investigate what would be people's opinion about its implementation in such an environment.

5. Social capital—the patterns of social behaviour and social institutions which facilitate interaction and exchange and the unity which holds a society together. Examples: links between farmers and markets or local forms of collective action and dispute resolution (Colleta and Nezam, 1998).

Measure f) in our questionnaire, concerns the support of entities which can identify political forces and groups favoring peace and long-term reconciliation and which can examine the benefits derived by certain groups from conflict and its perpetuation.

Development Cooperation Analyses

Finally, our third group of measures concerns two main ideas in development cooperation. The first one, relates to investments aimed at improving the capacity to cope with crisis, particularly among vulnerable groups. The example we presented to the interviewed people in Angola, involved giving instruments and seeds at the community level. The second measure involves the idea of granting micro-credit to individual persons or small enterprises in order to initiate or expand an economic activity.

Conflicts have devastating effects on the countries which face them. Some studies try to go even further and provide a clear understanding of the real consequences of conflicts. According to Stewart (1993) war is liable, at the macro level, to lead to falling output which translates to both market and public entitlements[6] reduction. At the meso level, there are strong downward influences

---

6. War is liable to lead to falling output, as a result of a combination of destruction of physical and human capital, reduced manpower following mobilisation and migration, destroyed or interrupted marketing and transport networks and reduced supplies of inputs both domestically produced (as a consequence of the general decline in output) and from abroad, because of foreign exchange shortages and/or embargoes. The reduction in gross national product (GNP), on the other hand, translates into reduction in both market and public entitlements. Market entitlements decline directly for the self-employed whose activities are interrupted by war. If food production falls, food marketing channels are disrupted and food imports reduced; rising food prices may lead to a sharp fall in food entitlements. Reduced public entitlements result from the various negative influences on output levels outlined above and from the decline of the levels of tax revenue with reduction in national income (Stewart: 1993).

on public resources for basic needs such as health and education facilities and food subsidies. Finally, the micro level or household level is the recipient of all negative effects arising at both the previous levels.

Further main costs can be identified such as the destruction of institutional capital and perhaps most critically, social and cultural capital. So, he concludes, that from the perspective of the human and economic implications, the view that development should be postponed until the wars are over is usually wrong for two main reasons. Firstly, it raises development costs of war, which is especially serious when the war is prolonged. It is usually advocated that war-torn countries hold back on all social and economic investments until the conflict has come to an end. However, such investments in these societies is where they are most needed. Secondly, in many situations some development projects are needed if relief is to be effective.[7] According to the author, development efforts are a 'waste of resources' only if projects are likely to be destroyed immediately. In addition, he also states that in order to avoid it, development efforts just need to be redesigned to become less vulnerable to attacks.[8]

Different studies give different arguments for the same line of thought. Commins (1996), for example, states that the new aid concepts do not view development as depending on the end of armed hostilities, because they include relations and capacities which require attention even during conflicts.

---

7. Example: in most cases relief cannot take place without some development efforts such as transport reconstruction (Stewart, 1993).

8. Examples: building minor, untarmacked roads, small airstrips, mobile schools and health posts, mini-energy projects, rather than massive projects which are obvious targets, as well as building small-scale dispersed industry rather than large centralised factories (Stewart, 1993).

We decided to include this contribution, even though the author believes that the costs of war can be reduced only by focused government action, due to what we consider to be relevant arguments in the context of the analysis.

Is it plausible to think, however, that in circumstances where the lack of basic needs is a constant fact and poverty is widespread due to the conflict situation, the population of these countries will think about the possibility of promoting development in their war-torn society?

Moreover, is it possible that they will consider the use of international aid to promote development as a priority in relation to the use of that same aid in humanitarian assistance or for the conflict resolution? These are two of the main aspects we will now analyze in the case study about Angola.

CHAPTER 4

METHODOLOGY

The methods used in this exploratory research were review of secondary sources, direct observation and semi-structured interviews (Mikkelsen, 1995). As far as the secondary sources are concerned, we did some research before departing and while in Angola. By analyzing the main theoretical contributions in the area of aid policy in war-torn countries we diagnosed the main questions of the research and established the basic theoretical background. On the other hand, the review of secondary sources of the country and the direct observation (as well as the interviews), allowed us to make relevant adaptations to the contents of the interviews, apart from giving us important knowledge for the analytical part of the research.

In order to create dialogue for collecting information, the main aim of the primary research, we used the semi-structured interviews method (see the interview in annex 1), following some of the basic principles of the Participatory Rural Appraisals (PRAs). Namely, the use of methods in a flexible way, seeking diversity and continuously making a self behavioural examination.[1] We used the informal conversational interview (30 interviews) and a formal open-ended interview (70 interviews) according to the specific

---

1. Self behavioural examination or self-critical awareness: 'meaning that facilitators (interviewers) are continuously examining their behaviour and trying to do better.' (Mikkelsen, 1995, p.69).

circumstances (Mikkelsen, 1995). We opted for a formal open-ended questionnaire conducted through semi-structured interviews in order to get in-depth responses and be able to explore the reasons for the answers given.[2] Moreover, unexpected relevant issues could also be followed up with further questions or probing.[3]

The interviews were all carried out personally, in the indigenous language (Portuguese), and presented to key individuals and homogeneous groups in what it is called chain of interviews (Mikkelsen, 1995). Moreover, the interviews were tape recorded as much as possible (41) and the full text, transcribed. Some were not recorded because people were reluctant to do it (4) while for others it was impossible because we were dealing with group interviews (18)[4]. Furthermore, due to external noises, sometimes recording was also not possible (7). We further believe that the willingness of the majority to let the interview be recorded had to do with the access established. There was an Angolan introducing us to some of the interviewed people and also being present when we were meeting most of the previously selected people. We should also consider that the confidentiality promised in terms of personal details may have contributed to that fact.

In terms of selection, we sought diversity, trying to talk to people from different age groups, from as many different professional areas and coming from different areas of the country as much as possible (see annex 2). We believed it to be important to have opinions from people who lived in Angola in peaceful times, people who have spent most of their adult lives facing war and young people whose perceptions are the perceptions of the future generation of the country. In relation to the professional areas we looked for opinions from people working in such different activity

---

2. Due to the limitations of this research we didn't include the analysis of the (30) informal conversational interviews .

3. Probing questions : 'direct questions that lead to key issues without beating around the bush' (Mikkelsen, 1995, p.75).

4. From this 18, we have 2 group interviews of 4 people and 2 group interviews of 5 people.

sectors as hospitals and schools, NGOs, government, private sector and media.

As far as the different areas of the country are concerned, we believe it to be important to have people coming from different areas of the country because those who have always lived in Luanda didn't directly suffer the military activities of the war (except for a few days in 1992). Finally, we tried to have a balanced sample in terms of gender (see annex 2). Due to the limitations of the kind of work we are doing it was not possible to include this detailed analysis in our case study.

The last brief discussion we would like to present concerns the main strengths and weaknesses of the research. One main weakness could be the non-representative character of the sample. However, as we are dealing with exploratory research, and even though we tried to interview a considerable number and diversity of people, we were not concerned about the percentage of people interviewed in relation to the estimated 12 million Angolan inhabitants. Secondly, having 18 (out of 70 interviews analyzed in this particular study) interviews as group interviews could also be pointed out as a weakness. Nevertheless, in the big majority of the cases, we didn't find that people's answers were influenced by the opinions of each other. In fact, they would openly disagree and state their arguments. Additionally, the dynamics of group interviews tend to pave the way for unexpected questions and provide additional information. Thirdly, the fact that the 70 interviews analyzed in this study were all done to people with high school or university education can also represent a weakness. On the other hand, what we found was that people without this kind of education were not able to understand the main questions of the research (those presented in the section—development in conflict situations). We have several cases like this in the 30 informal conversational interviews.

Fourthly, the fact that some of the measures proposed for being implemented in Angola at the moment (section on recent findings on aid policy—part II), were too conceptual, led, in some circumstances, to limitations in terms of the comprehension of the questions. The last two weaknesses we would like to point out relate to the time and resource constraints to follow up further research and the personal biases of the interviewer.

In terms of main strengths, we would like to emphasize the combination of the different methods used. Firstly, as seen earlier, the previous analysis of secondary sources allowed for diagnosing, in advance, the main questions of the research and the establishment of the basic theoretical background. Both of them were then appraised with the primary research. Secondly, the analysis, on the field, of secondary sources and the direct observation enabled for relevant adaptations to the contents of the interviews being made, apart from constituting important knowledge for the analytical part of the research. Thirdly, as far as the semi-structured interviews are concerned, the use of open-ended questionnaires allowed us to obtain in depth-responses and to be able to explore people's reactions to our questions as well as the justifications for the answers given. Moreover, unexpected relevant issues could also be followed up with further questions. Fourthly, in order to create dialogue for collecting information, the access mentioned before was crucial for building up a relationship with people and putting them at ease to discuss the issues raised by the research. Finally, we would like to mention the diversity of the interviewed people and the fact that by asking the same questions of the respondents, the comparability of responses was increased, facilitating organization and the analysis of the data.

PART II
THE CASE STUDY

CHAPTER 5

ANGOLA: THE COUNTRY

Angola is situated in the Western region of Southern Africa. It is the fifth biggest country in Sub-Saharan Africa with a territory of 1.246.700 Km2, a coast of 1.650 Km and 4.837 Km of land frontier. The great majority of 12 million inhabitants that are estimated to form the population of Angola come from people of Bantu origin. The annual growth rate of population is evaluated at 2.8 per cent with the majority of the population (45 per cent) being under 14 years old. It is also assessed that more than 60 per cent of the population is living in the main urban areas (PNUD, 1997).

In terms of natural resources the great diversity in Angola is the main richness of the country. The mineral resources are on the top of the scale, leaving petroleum as the leader followed by the diamonds. There are also other mineral resources such as iron, manganese, copper, phosphate, granite, marble and rare minerals. With a coast of 1.650 Km, Angola has also a rich sea in fish, mollusc and crustaceans. The forest resources are other richnesses, with wood of great economic value such as black-wood, rare-wood, iron-wood, ebony and African sandalwood (PNUD, 1997).

Angola achieved its independence from the Portuguese rule in 1975 after 14 years of armed struggle. After independence, the armed struggle continued between the main political factions,

M.P.L.A.[1] and U.N.I.T.A.[2] There have been several attempts at peace settlement, namely the 1992 Bicesse Agreement, which resulted in the first democratic elections, and the 1994 Lusaka Agreement. However, none of them have produced results and the civil war is still ongoing until today.

Furthermore, in the 1997 Angolan Human Development Report we find further interesting data. It was estimated that around 67 per cent of the urban population lived below the poverty line in 1996; more than 40 per cent of poor household leaders were women with most of them having more than 5 children and only 12 per cent of the population was having a stable job. In terms of income distribution, the Report mentions that the richest 10 per cent received 30 per cent of the country's income while the poorest 10 per cent received only 2.2 per cent. In the urban areas the Gini Coefficient was 0.40 per cent, also showing the high degree of disparity in terms of income distribution (PNUD, 1997). Finally, we would just like to draw your attention to the following tables and graphic, showing the budget tendencies and human deprivation index. This data is particularly relevant for our subsequent analysis.

Table 1. Budget Tendencies of Angola Between 1992 and 1995

	1992	1993	1994	1995
Current expenditures	5.002	2.865	2.653	3.332
Defense and security	958	1.414	1.578	1.742
Social sector	507	364	167	181
Interest rates	476	498	429	727
Revenues	2.057	2.065	1.708	1.848
Ratio Defense expenditures/ revenues	0.47	0.68	0.92	0.94

---

1. MPLA (Movimento Popular de Libertação de Angola).
2. UNITA (União Nacional para Independência Total de Angola).

Source: We translated the Portuguese version found in the 1997 Angolan Human Development Report.

As we can see there was an increase, between 1994 and 1995, of 26 per cent in expenditures for the defense and security sector. On the other hand, since 1992 until 1995 there was a decrease of 64% in expenditures in the social sector, which was already receiving in 1992 almost half of the investments made in the defense and security sector.

Table 2. Human Deprivation Index of Angola in 1996

	Urban Areas	Rural Areas	Angola
Human Deprivation Index	53.2	64.2	59
Life expectancy (years)	44	41	42
Illiteracy rate (%)	40.4	58.1	50.9
4 or more people for each bedroom (%) (a)	15.7	24.5	20.8
Population with no access to water	47.8	76.5	64.7
Malnourishment of children under 5 years old (%)	4.8	7	6.4

Source: We translated and changed graphically the Portuguese version found in the 1997 Angolan Human Development Report.

(a) The indicator relating to access to health services was substituted by the rate of occupation of household rooms due to the lack of data. This indicator shows the implications that congested households may have on the population health, especially, on what disease infection is concerned.

Graphic 1. Human Deprivation Index of Angola in 1996.

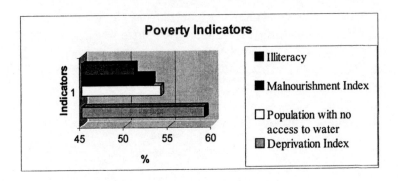

Source: we translated and changed graphically the Portuguese version found in the 1997 Angolan Human Development Report.

As shown in both table and graphic, the human deprivation index for Angola is 59 per cent, meaning that 59 per cent of the Angolan population was, in 1996, affected by several forms of human poverty. Furthermore, this index placed Angola among the four worst countries at the world level (with Burkina Faso, Sierra Leone and Niger).

In relation to the Pearson Coefficient[3] of illiteracy rate and human deprivation index among the several provinces of the country, the Report estimated a correlation of 0.99, which means that if the regions were disposed according to the illiteracy rate or by the index itself, the results would be the same. The Report, then concludes that Education is one crucial priority in terms of conceiving development policies.

---

3. Correlation coefficient which assesses the relation between two sets of data. It assumes figures in the interval of (-1) (no relation) to (+1) (maximum relation).

CHAPTER 6

DEVELOPMENT IN CONFLICT
SITUATIONS

One of the main questions of the primary research is, precisely, related to the doubt of whether people living in a war-torn country would believe in the possibility of promoting development in a conflict situation and why. In the case of Angola the results were the following ones: the great majority of the interviewed people in Angola answered positively to that possibility in their country. From the 67 answers obtained, 47 (70 per cent) believed that to be possible in Angola, while only 20 (30 per cent) believed it not to be possible.[1] The arguments supporting the answers were quite broad. Among the positive answers some said that it is possible to promote development with the country in war because that's what has been happening (2 answers).[2] Others said that there are measures which contribute to the development of the country and that can be implemented even though the country is in war (2

---

1. From the yes group 13 answers are group answers and from the no group 4 answers are also group answers.
2. The persons who answered this way were involved, one with the governmental activities and another one was involved with an education project that has been extending itself successfully for several regions of the country.

answers); while others answered that there are development areas in which investments can be made which will then contribute to the global development when the war is finished (1 answer). However, the most frequent answer (15) mentions that this development would be possible only in the areas not directly affected by the war. In relation to this last point, a careful analysis is necessary in order to identify possible consequences of promoting some kind of investments in some areas while neglecting others, in a country where the concentration of the population may be one main reason contributing to its underdevelopment. The same applies to one answer which pointed out the creation of secured areas where that development would be pursued without alarm.

We also have a significant number of people (10 answers in 47—21 per cent) who didn't give any justification, only mentioning, on the second part of the question, what would be the measures to promote that development. As far as the negative answers are concerned 5 main justifications were given. 4 (from 20) people believed development to be impossible in their country in a war-torn context due to the concentration of population in the main urban areas; 3 alluded to the lack of communication between the majority of the regions inside the country while 2 brought up 3 other explanations. The first one is the impossibility of promoting agriculture. The second one, the lack of national resources as they are mostly used for the war. Finally, the third one draws our attention to the concept of development. For 2 of those that answered in a negative way to this question development is about a multiplicity of factors that can not be promoted while the country is in war. Furthermore, for these 2 Angolans, what the donor agencies could do is invest in some key sectors that will show its potentiality for the rapid development of the country when the war will be over. As it happened with the positive answers also in this case we had a significant number of answers without justification (6 answers in 20—30 per cent). As we can see two main points come out of this analysis. Firstly, that there is a strong belief in the possibility of promoting development in Angola with the war, especially in areas not directly involved in the conflict effort.

Secondly, that the arguments presented in both positive and negative answers are quite broad.

Moreover, we questioned the interviewed people about which measures should be taken with the international aid in order for war-torn development in Angola to be achieved.

In the case of the negative answers we ask them where would they invest the international aid even though the development of the country was not possible at that moment. The broad results are shown in table 3, whereas the specific measures are presented in table 5. The columns yes and no refer to those who answered yes and no to the possibility of promoting development in a conflict situation. We will analyze the relevance of this distinction afterwards.

Table 3. Sectors of Investment for the International Aid

Sector	Yes (from 43)	No (from 19)	Total (from 62)
Education	36	12	48
Health	18	7	25
Agriculture	9	3	12
Public Infrastructure	6	4	10
Industry	5	3	8
Fisheries	1	1	2
Culture	-	1	1
International organizations	3	2	5
Human rights	1	1	2
Humanitarian aid	10	6	16
Conflict resolution	-	1	1

Note: these are aggregated results. Even when two or more measures of a particular activity sector were proposed by the same person they only count as one, exactly, because we are considering activity sectors for investment.

By looking at the table we can retain three main conclusions. Firstly, that education and health are considered priority areas for investing the international aid (77 per cent answered education and 40 per cent answered health, while only 19 per cent answered agriculture, the third more frequent answer).

Even those who discard the possibility of pursuing development in a conflict situation, believe it to be important to maintain investments, especially in the education sector, while the country is facing the conflict (63 per cent comparing with 37 per cent who answered health, the second more common answer). This way, they justify, 'we are planning and investing on our future development.' Education seems to be particularly relevant as people realize that the massive dislocations of people to the big cities translate in a very significant number of children and young people staying outside school for several years (especially if we think of Angola as a country in civil war for more than 25 years). As seen in the previous section, the Pearson Coefficient of illiteracy rate and human deprivation index in 1996 entirely sustains these findings. Secondly, we should pay some attention to the fact that people from both groups have basically the same ideas as to how the international aid should be invested. There seems to be a shared vision of what is necessary and in which degree, the only difference being that some believe these investments would translate in development in current circumstances while the others don't. Thirdly, there are a significant number of people saying that in order for the international aid to promote development in Angola, even though the country is in war, it should be invested in humanitarian aid (10 answers—23 per cent—from the yes group).[3] What

---

3. We don't consider the 6 answers from the no group because it is not surprising that people who don't believe in the possibility of pursuing development in a war context, think that the international aid should go for humanitarian aid. On the other hand, people from the yes group were specifically asked about investments with international aid that would promote development.

comes out from these answers is a concept of development that incorporates humanitarian aid.

The first conclusion we just made can be further emphasized by the next data.

Table 4. Priority Sectors for Investing the International Aid

Priority Sector	Yes	No	Total
Education	27	7	34
Health	5	2	7
Agriculture	2	-	2
Industry	1	-	1
Public Infrastructure	-	1	1
Organization of the state	1	-	1
Human rights	1	-	1
Humanitarian aid	4	2	6
Conflict resolution	-	1	1

As it is shown in the table, especially education, but also health, are the priorities of people for investing international aid in Angola, even for those in the no group. The interesting thing in relation to these results is that people were not asked about priority sectors for investing the international aid. They spontaneously referred them.

However, let's analyze in more detail what were the specific measures proposed. We found it interesting to present this fifth table, firstly, because there are some measures excluded from the first table due to the problem of inserting them on the right sector. Secondly, some measures are quite peculiar and we believe this way the reader will have an open field of analysis.

Table 5. Measures Proposed for Investing the International Aid

Measure	Yes	No	Total
Education sector	28	11	39
Build schools	17	4 (a)	21
Training teachers	9 (b)	1	10
Creation of professional schools	6 (c)	1	7
Workshops, conferences, seminars about national problems	4	1	5
Adult literacy	3	-	3
Build infant schools	1	1	2
Promote sanitary education	2	-	2
Bring foreign teachers	1	-	1
Supply food to schools for both teachers and students	1	-	1
Promote health education about the main epidemics	1	-	1
Promote agriculture education	1	-	1
Support scientific research	1	-	1
Schools infrastructure rehabilitation	1	-	1
Supply of didactic material	1	-	1
Build libraries	1	-	1
Promote schools assessments	1	-	1
Health sector	13	5	18
Build hospitals	4	3	7
Build health centers	3 (d)	2	5
Promote better primary health care	3	1	4
Health infrastructure and equipment rehabilitation	3	-	3
Medicines for the epidemics	1	1	2
Promote child health access	1	-	1
Training nurses	1	-	1
Training specialized doctors	1	-	1
Encourage national doctors abroad to return	1	-	1
	1	-	1

Measure	Yes	No	Total
Promote hospitals and health centers assessments			
Agriculture sector	8 (e)	3	11
Supply seeds and instruments	1	-	1
Infrastructure sector	2 (f)	-	1
Build roads	4	2	6
Build bridges	3	1	4
Promote basic sanitation	1	1	2
Promote public transports	2	-	2
Industry sector	4 (g)	-	4
Stimulate the creation of industries	1	1	2
Promote the handicrafts production	1 (h)	1	2
Support to the small and medium enterprises	-	1	1
Support to the media	3	-	3
Fisheries sector	1	1	2
Tourism sector	1	-	1
Support cultural institutions such as museums, libraries, archives.	-	1	1
Training cultural human resources	-	1	1
Support the creation of a dramatic arts school	-	1	1
Support the theater groups	1	-	1
Support the aid agencies understanding of socio-economic realities of each Angolan region	1	2 (i)	3
Support the clear definition of aid funds	1	-	1
Support the coordination of aid agencies	1	-	1

Measure	Yes	No	Total
Promote aid funds assessments	1	-	1
Promote the protection of the child	1	1	2
Promote the protection of women	-	1	1
Support the organization of the government and the communities	1	-	1
Support the creation of a management production system	1	-	1
Demining	-	1	1
Support job creation	2	-	2
Mobilize funds for the return and reintegration of refugees	1	1	2
Humanitarian aid	10	6	16
Support the resolution of the conflict		1	2

(a) One person referred this to be particularly important in rural areas.

(b) One alluded to this training in the professional areas.

(c) 2 people mentioned the importance of this kind of education for the military men while one specifically considered this kind of education to be very important in the rural areas and in the fields of agriculture and transforming industry.

(d) One answer points out the especial need of these health centers in the surroundings of the main cities.

(e) 2 interviewed people draw their attention to the importance of this measure in how the food security of households is concerned. Which leads an open question as to how this can be promoted.

(f) One answer specifically relates to the support of self-construction projects.

(g) One person mentions credit to the industry.

(h) This person specifically considered the promotion of credit to these producers.

(i) One person was thinking particularly of identifying the causes of problems in the several regions.

A detailed analysis of the table leads us to several conclusions. Firstly, people seem to agree with some conclusions made by the 1998 World Bank Report. Namely, the idea that the role of aid in difficult environments is to educate the next generation of leaders, disseminate information about policy and stimulate public debate[4]. Moreover, also the idea that many of the measures that promote long-term growth, such as that basic education helps reduce poverty, seems to be reinforced. This can be seen by the emphasis given on education in the last three tables. In relation to this point, I would like to recall some ideas by Joyner (1996)[5]. The majority of the Angolan people interviewed appear to share the view that improved education and training is an investment in people which can survive physical destruction. Furthermore, it is important to build on the existing involvement of communities to support school education, as is the case. In addition, there seems to be a common view on two further aspects. On the one hand, that schools are symbolic of a return to some form of recognizable routine and are the ideal forum for reaching war affected children and adults. On the other hand, teachers are respected members of their communities and if we raise their awareness of the importance of such issues as health, girls' education and psycho-social needs we are giving a crucial first step to long-term and culturally appropriate development in these fields.

Secondly, the current idea that dealing with refugees is an early reconstruction or post-conflict settlement issue (Bakwesegha,

---

4. The second and third points are reinforced by the answers to measure e) in the case study.

5. Even though she refers to these aspects as important aspects to be taken into account by agencies promoting relief support.

1998; Colleta and Nezam, 1998; OECD/DAC, 1998) doesn't seem to be shared by some people.

The same applies to repair of communications, de-mining (Colleta and Nezam, 1998) and large scale employment generating projects (OECD/DAC, 1998). As we can see in the table, people have proposed these measures to be implemented while the conflict is ongoing.

In this context, it is relevant to analyze Agerbak's (1991) contribution to the debate. In the author's analysis of how aid programmes grow and change in emergency situations, it is stated that from the experience of development agencies, there is a consolidation stage (at least three years after the conflict has started) in which programmes progress beyond crisis into an effort to address development in conflict. In this third stage, programmes acquire characteristics such as long-term planning, socio-economic assessments, institution building, technical training, increasing self-reliance among others. As we know, the Angolan civil war is ongoing for more than 25 years and the interviewed people seem to believe that this stage was reached long time ago.

Moreover, in relation to the different types of emergency assistance in complex political emergencies, we would like to add another point. Perhaps we should consider the possibility of war-torn countries facing different needs at the same time, in terms of emergency assistance. According to the regions of the countries, we may find higher need, in some of them, for relief assistance while in others development assistance could be a priority. This appears to be particularly relevant in countries which can represent, for example, several European countries in terms of territory.

Due to the fact that people could have answered positively to the question of whether it is possible to pursue development in Angola with the conflict ongoing, while at the same time believing that the priority for investing the international aid would be humanitarian aid or conflict resolution, we decided to add another question. We decided to ask people about which field was a priority for the international aid to be invested at that moment. Whether in the case of Angola aid should focus on the resolution of the conflict, on humanitarian aid or on the social and economic development (question no. 7). The results are shown in table 6.

Table 6. Priority Field of Intervention
for the International Aid

Field of Intervention	Yes (from 42)	No (from 19)	Total (from 61)
Social and economic development	33	11	44+3 (a) = 47
Humanitarian aid	17	13	30+2 (b) = 32
Conflict resolution	20	9	29
Total	42 (c)	19 (d)	

Note: the columns yes and no refer to those who answer yes and no to the possibility of pursuing development in a conflict situation.

(a) The 3 that we added relates to 1 person who didn't answer question 4 on the questionnaire but answered question 7 saying social and economic development and 2 more who in the same situation answered humanitarian aid and development.

(b) Once more we added here the 2 answers relating to those who didn't answer question 4 but that in question 7 said humanitarian aid and development.

(c) We have 7 people answering all the three fields of intervention, another 7 answering both humanitarian aid and social and economic development, 4 people answering social and economic development and conflict resolution and 1 answering conflict resolution and humanitarian aid. We thought it would be better in terms of analysis to aggregate the results.

(d) We have 5 people answering all the three fields of intervention and 4 persons answering both humanitarian aid and social and economic development.

This analysis shows itself important for the following reasons. Firstly, we can conclude how many of those (47 people) who believed in the possibility of promoting development in a war context, actually think that investing international aid on that field is a priority. In this case we have a significant number (33 answers—70 per cent). The justification given most of the time is that the international aid can't promote the resolution of the conflict and that humanitarian aid, apart from generating dependency and leading to a loss of working habits, is a short-term investment which can not promote long-term development. On the other hand, even though the social and economic development field didn't obtain the highest rate of answers in the no group, which is also quite understandable, it's actually very close to the other fields. We have 11 persons (from 19—58 per cent) thinking that investments in the field of social and economic development, even though not promoting development, are important while the war is ongoing for the future development of the country. As we can see in the total results, the social and economic development field is actually the first priority for these Angolans in terms of aid investment (77 per cent, compared with 52 per cent who answered humanitarian aid, the second more frequent answer). Thirdly, we have a considerable number of people (29 answers—47,5 per cent) who still show reliance on the international aid to promote the resolution of the conflict, even after several failed attempts.

Additionally, we cannot neglect some inconsistencies obtained through a detailed comparison of the answers of the no group for the 4th and 7th questions. We have 8 answers which didn't mention investments in humanitarian aid in the 4th question (when they were asked where should international aid be invested) but did it on the 7th question.

We have other 4 answers on the same circumstances but relating to conflict resolution. Finally, we have 1 answer mentioning humanitarian aid in the 4th and conflict resolution in the 7th question[6].

In order to make a final evaluation of the importance, for the interviewed people, of promoting social and economic development in Angola, even though the country is facing a war for more than 25 years, we asked them what should the priority field for investing the international aid in the 1980s have been. The results are shown in table 7.

Table 7. Priority Field of Intervention for the International Aid in the 1980s.

Field of Intervention	Yes (from 16)	No (from 7)	Total (from 24)
Social and economic development	12	4	16+1= 17 (a)
Humanitarian aid	2	3	5
Conflict resolution	4	1	5
Total	16 (b)	7 (c)	

(a) We add one person who didn't answer question 4 because it can't be included in either group.

(b) We have 1 person saying both social and economic development and conflict resolution and another one answering humanitarian aid and social and economic development.

(c) We have 1 person answering both humanitarian aid and social and economic development.

---

6. Our conjecture is that people would state the most important areas of investment on the 4th question, even though they are not asked about priorities. However, we also bear in mind that a conflict situation is not the appropriate time to expect logical answers.

Even though our number of answers decreased significantly for various reasons[7], it was interesting to see the results especially when compared with the answers given in the previous question. The first point to highlight is, as in the previous table, the significant number of people who believed the social and economic development field of intervention to be the priority for investing the international aid also in the 1980s (17 answers from a total of 24 - 71 per cent). Secondly, there seems to be an increasing need for these investments to be used in humanitarian aid and conflict resolution as time passes by. We just have to compare the results in table 6 with the results in table 7. Thirdly, when establishing the comparison between question 7 and 8 (table 6 and 7) we find the following results: 12 people changed their opinion and reinforced the role of social and economic development intervention at that time; 4 people did the same in relation to the conflict resolution field and only 2 in relation to humanitarian aid. There were some explanations for that. On the one hand, people realized the permanent degradation of life conditions and think that investments in social and economic development since that time would have translated in better conditions at the moment. On the other hand, most people believed that humanitarian aid was not such a necessity in the 1980s. The conflict didn't have the dimension it assumed afterwards and most people were still able to farm for subsistence. Moreover, some believed that the conflict could have been resolved at that time if things would have been done in different ways.

---

7. The main reasons were the fact that many people didn't want to answer and many others couldn't do it due to their age.

CHAPTER 7
RECENT FINDINGS ON AID POLICY

Another important contribution for the discussion would be to ask people whether they had confidence in the likely effectiveness of the measures we selected from different studies. Before starting the analysis we would like, however, to remind that all these measures were proposed to people as measures to be implemented while the country is in war. The three main ideas that come out of this analysis are the general support to the measures, the several ideas given to implement them and the fact that these are not seen as priority areas of investment. Even though people generally think of the measures as good ideas and that its implementation would translate in benefits to the country and their lives, giving several interesting ideas how to put them in practice, these measures don't coincide with the priorities they established in the previous section.

Going back to the theoretical analysis, the first measure we decided to include was World Bank's (1998) proposal of support to reform minded elements in the society and the government. According to the Report, development aid should, in high distorted environments, support knowledge creation in the sense of financing and evaluating innovations. This would further mean helping reformers develop and test their ideas.

In the case study, the majority of the interviewed people answered positively to the implementation of this measure in Angola (23 out of 28—82 per cent), while only 2 answered negatively. From the positive answers, the first aspect we would like to emphasize is the several meanings given by people to reform minded elements, probably already identifying the reform elements they believe to exist in Angola. Examples are the political opposition, civil society, independent individuals, political and civil associations, private media or private economic agents.

The second aspect we would like to highlight is that a significant number (8—28,5 per cent) of those who answered in a positive or negative way didn't seem to understand the question in its meaning, justifying their answer with arguments as 'yes, because every associations have reform in their minds.' On the other hand, some interesting ideas came out, such as, that aid agencies should view political opposition in an alternative, empowering way and not just as having a critical role in relation to the political party in power. Furthermore, that a kind of national conference, with these reform minded elements, should be supported in order to analyze the future development of the country. In addition, some answers also refer that this kind of support should be given to these elements who are interested in broadening the political, economical and social debate among the society. As far as the negative answers are concerned, we had one person saying no because it would mean getting involved in the internal politics of the country and another one answering negatively because these reforming persons could be seen as foreign agents. Apart from the ideas given, the two main points coming out of this analysis are the following ones. On one hand, almost half[1] (46 per cent) of the people didn't understand the meaning of the question. Perhaps it was too abstract and people couldn't think of its applicability in reality. This can be seen on the fact that no answer gives a practical way of implementing this measure. On the other hand, only few people (2) thought of this measure as being really important for the development of their country at that time.

---

1. The 8 that we mentioned plus the 2 negative answers (as we can see from the justifications), and the 3 that we didn't consider as answering positive or negative.

The second measure proposed by the World Bank Report refers to engaging civil society in the provision of services, namely to pressure the government to change or to take service provision directly into civil society's own hands. We will not analyze it in detail as the main conclusion is that most people didn't understand it. Once more we relate this to a level of abstraction of the question as well as to the problems encountered in implementing civil society's literature. What kind of pressure to the government is the World Bank thinking of, or how can civil society take service provision into its own hands are two general doubts. On the other hand, this level of abstraction may be needed in theoretical works so that adaptations to the several country specific characteristics are possible. One of the very few answers, from someone working on a national NGO, emphasized the importance of the measure especially in such a big country. According to the answer, in these countries the State is not always able to assume its role everywhere and in each circumstance, and civil society can fill this space.

On the second group of analysis, as we recall, we referred to measures proposed by different conflict analysis studies. The first one was Bakwesegha's (1998) idea of teaching people the meaning of democratic institutions, how to defend them and how to use them as tools for absorbing conflicts. The results of the case study were the following ones: 30 answers (88 per cent) in favor and 1 against the implementation of such a measure in Angola (on a total of 34). Furthermore, the negative answer was given without any justification. Turning to the positive answers, the first point we would like to highlight, is the belief of many of the interviewed people (8—23,5 per cent) that there is no democratic regime in Angola at that moment.

Secondly, the ways put forward to implement this measure were the following ones: through education (4 answers), through the training of those working on these institutions (3 answers), courses or seminars (3 answers) and through the media (2 answers). The last three measures have further interesting specific ideas. For 3 of the interviewed people it is important to promote the training of people working for the democratic institutions because there is a real need that these people give the example to the rest of the population. Moreover, according to them, these civil servants really need that knowledge in a country lacking democratic history and which has lived the passage to a 'supposed democracy' in a very sudden way. To notice that this training of government officials is precisely one measure proposed by the 1998 World Bank Report[2]. In what applies to the courses or seminars and media, two further interesting observations were made. On the one hand, the courses or seminars should be done by national institutions and in all the national languages. On the other hand, the media are a valuable source, as long as they reach the entire population which doesn't happen in Angola. Another point to retain from the answers is the unwillingness by some of them (4) that the western model of democracy is adopted on their country, due to the specific characteristics of Angola. This reason further leads to a correlation with the educational way of promoting democracy. For some of the interviewed people, the population needs to acquire the democratic values through the several educational processes in life, and only after this can maturely decide on which regime is more appropriate for their country. As one of them said: ' Democracy is not something you can do on the paper. People start acquiring, since they are born, specific kinds of rules and through the several education processes they will find the political regime more appropriate to their specific realities.' Once more, apart from the ideas given, three main conclusions were retained. Firstly, the almost unanimous support to the measure. It seems that many people believe in some of the values behind a democratic political regime. Secondly, the fact that a significant number of people (23,5 per cent) clearly stated the non-existence

---

2. On chapter 4—Aid can be the midwife of good institutions—of the 1998 World Bank Policy Research Report, one of the measures proposed on the non-financial support section was, precisely, training government officials. This measure was not, however, included on the analysis for high distorted environments. Furthermore, it was not mentioned any specific kind of training as in the case study answer.

of democracy in Angola at that moment and also that some of them (12 per cent) clearly rejected the western model of democracy. Thirdly, we also have to note that, contrary to what happened with the first two measures, people were able to mention practical ways of using the aid in this context.

The second measure on the second group of analysis—measure d) on the questionnaire—relates to the importance of reinforcing civil society and social capital. In order to do this, Scharf (1998) proposed the support of institutions such as citizens' advice bureau and national and local media. In the primary research we obtained 42 answers (out of 50—84 per cent) pro support of citizens' advice bureau[3], 24 pro support of national and local media[4] and 2 answers against the channeling of international aid to the support of citizens' advice bureau. We found no one opposing the support of the national and local media. The negative answers were given on the basis that it would be a misuse of resources and that people are well informed, their problem being the lack of conditions to live along those lines.

In terms of the support to citizens' advice bureau (8 people) believed that it should go to health advice institutions, (5 people) to legal advice institutions, (4 people) to economic advice institutions, (3 people) to civic and human rights advice institutions and (3 people) to women victims of violence advice institutions. But let's analyze which are the prominent measures in each field. In relation to the health advice institutions, people emphasized advice for preventing the main diseases (which is deeply related with hygiene issues), and advice for family planning. As far as the legal advice is concerned, they emphasized the need for this to be widespread all over the country and one person also suggested the elaboration of cards with legal messages in all the national

---

3. 3 out of the 42 answers in favor of supporting citizens' advice bureau were group answers.

4. 5 out of the 24 answers in favor of supporting national and local media were group answers.

languages. On the economic field, people mentioned the need for advice on the importance of savings for investment and how to manage economic activities. Moreover, some further believed this advice to be one main component of school education. According to some of them it is worthless to advise uneducated people on these matters as those who don't understand the advice will not adopt them in their daily behaviors. Another interesting point referred to, was the importance of having the conditions for the advice to be implemented by people (3 answers, 2 from the yes group and 1 from the no group). There was even one person who, while thinking about the traditional Angolan communities, proposed that these advice institutions should find young people from the communities, who, having some kind of education, would be willing to become a vehicle of introduction of this advice to the communities (always bearing in mind the importance of the community leader authorization).

In terms of the support to national and local media, one interesting result that came out of the answers was peoples' opinion about the main role of media for the development of the country.

Four (4) answers illustrate them as key instruments for having information, (3) answers for promoting democracy while (2) emphasized its role in promoting the freedom of expression. Furthermore, we had (5) people saying this support should go for the private media as the public media are controlled by the government. Additionally, we had (2) people actually thinking of specific measures in relation to this support. Two answers mention the training of media professionals while (1) mentions the credit for the media in order for them to improve their information, the support for the creation of a television private sector in Angola and for the creation of professional media associations. Not surprisingly this last person believed this support to the media to be a priority in terms of investing the international aid.

We would like to emphasize three points in relation to the answers for this measure. On the one hand, as seen on the previous analysis, people were greatly positive about this measure in terms of support not only to citizens' advice bureau but also in terms of support to national and local media. On the other hand, they were also able to identify specific areas of intervention. Thirdly, it is also interesting to note that people, in the case of the citizens' advice bureau, identified quite a broad number of areas where they believe there is a lack of information. However, we should also bear in mind the issues that the absence of specification about organizational aspects of the bureau, may rise. We should think of the possibility, in people's mind, of thinking that the medical advice, for example, should be given in hospitals or health centers.

The third measure in the second group of analysis related to the need for agencies to develop an understanding of the context, dynamics and assistance needs of war-torn societies, in order to design appropriate interventions when conditions permit—measure e) on the questionnaire.

The results were: 29 (out of 32 answers—90 per cent) supporting the measure while only (2) answers didn't support it. An important aspect was that one of the no answers was precisely given by someone having a key role on one of the most trustworthy (according to people's opinion) national NGOs. The importance of the answer reflects its justification. He argued that these studies, in the case of Angola, are done and have been constantly updated, mainly by nationals. The fact is that the international organizations most of the times don't worry about making or having these studies by establishing previous contacts, especially with existent national organizations, to find out what is already done. The other no answer also refers to the existence of the studies and the waste of resources if more money would be spent on it. On the other hand, the majority of the interviewed (29—90 per cent) believe these studies to be very important for the success of the aid interventions. In fact they consider that aid agencies lack knowledge about the specific dynamics and characteristics of the country and its population. Furthermore, we would like to note here, the general scepticism of people in terms of the aid agencies interventions. Several specific criticisms were done: (2) answers mention the fact that the projects seem to reflect more aid agencies objectives than the national ones, (2) mentioned the lack of coordination within agencies themselves and with the government (which has an important know-how to share, namely the knowledge of the most important areas and measures to be implemented). On the opposite side, (2) answers also mention the national corruption as one factor to be taken into account. In conclusion, there is a need to highlight two points. First of all, the measure seems to be considered, by the majority of people, important to be implemented at that moment in Angola. Especially for the success of aid interventions to become a reality.

However, another question has to be raised. Is it possible that most of the interviewed people don't know if these studies are already done or not?[5] Probably it is difficult for people to conceive the existence of these studies and the ignorance of the same when interventions are to be made. In this particular case it would mean that aid resources shouldn't be spent on these studies and a re-evaluation of donors agencies interventions should be made. Secondly, we have to note the criticisms done by most of the people to the interventions of donor agencies.

The last measure on this group of analysis is OECD/DAC (1998) proposal of support to entities which can identify political forces and groups favoring peace and long-term reconciliation and which can examine the benefits derived by certain groups from the conflict and its perpetuation. Firstly, all interviewed people understood the question not only in terms of identifying the agents favoring peace and reconciliation and the benefits derived by certain groups from conflict and its perpetuation, but also in terms of supporting these agents on their interventions. Having this in mind, the results were the following ones: from the 37 answers

---

5. One of the two persons who said that the studies are already done is precisely the only person who is in direct contact with the aid cooperation environment, through the work on a national NGO.

obtained, 27 (73 per cent) supported the measure[6] while 8 (21 per cent) didn't. In terms of analysis, an interesting point is the high number of people who believe it is very difficult for this measure to have success in Angola (12 answers—32 per cent, 4 of which supported the measure). The reasons pointed out for this belief vary. The first justification concerns the fact that the aid already given has not shown any results (4 answers).

The second reasoning relates to the fact that the interested parties on the war would not allow anything to be done for the peace and reconciliation of the country (3 answers). Moreover, 2 answers mention the difficulty to identify those agents, as everyone claims to be one. Finally, (1) person believes that everything possible was already done to achieve peace and reconciliation and there were no results. Therefore, any investment in this field would be pointless. Among those who still believed something can be done in the name of peace and long-term reconciliation (10 people—27 per cent), 4 answers mentioned the importance of promoting a culture of peace and reconciliation among the population, even though peace may not be achieved this way. The means proposed to cultivate that culture were: seminars or conferences (3 answers); programs and articles in the media (3 answers); through education (2 answers); propaganda material (1 answer) and public manifestations (1 answer). Two main ideas should be kept from this analysis. Firstly, the high number of people (12 answers out of 24—50 per cent, if we discount the 13 answers without justification) who don't believe the measure could actually show positive results in Angola, even though it would be important to be implemented. Several obstacles seem to be in place for the success of these kind of measures. Secondly, the important idea that even though peace and reconciliation may not be possible to be achieved with international aid, donor agencies should remember the importance of promoting a culture of peace and

---

6. From this 27 answers 13 were given just by saying 'yes' with no further justification.

reconciliation among the population. Several ways were, further, put forward in order to do this.

As far as the third group of measures is concerned, relating to main ideas in development cooperation, we decided to include two additional measures.

The first one we will analyze refers to investments aimed at improving the capacity to cope with crisis, particularly among vulnerable groups. The example given concerned providing seeds and instruments at the community level. The results were the following ones: 41 (out of 45 answers—91 per cent) in favor[7] and 3 against the implementation of the measure in Angola while the country is in war. The initial point we would like to make concerns two of the justifications for the negative answers. The first justification was given on the basis that there is the need to reorganize the commercial network before implementing such a measure. The second justification was grounded on the fact that this measure doesn't create working habits. As we can see the correlation of the answers with the initial question is very weak. The third justification mentions corruption as a factor for not wasting aid resources on that field. However, the weak correlation with the question, especially in how the improvement of the capacity of communities to cope with crisis is concerned, can also be seen in the other group of answers. We have 3 people saying that the measure is important in order to promote national food self-sufficiency and 1 saying that this measure is important to promote the exports of primary products, having the international terms of trade to be revised. Other interesting points raised were that aid agencies or donors should demand something in return, such as a percentage of the production (3 answers). Additionally, according to 3 answers, for some communities there is a need to give food at the same time as the provision of seeds and instru-

---

7. From the 41 answers favoring the implementation of this measure, 17 just answered 'yes' without any justification. Furthermore, 2 were group answers.

ments, otherwise the seeds would be eaten. Moreover, aid agencies should first teach the communities how to produce their own stocks of seeds (2 answers). Furthermore, seeds and instruments should be given to communities according to what they are traditionally used to produce (2 answers).

The two last ideas concern the fact that aid agencies should be concerned at the same time with the question of mined fields (2 answers) and with the fact that better and national seeds should be given, because sometimes foreign seeds don't produce any result (1 answer). Finally, we would like to mention that 4 people clearly stated their preference for this kind of aid in relation to humanitarian aid. The two main points of the analysis are, firstly, the support of the majority of the people for that measure to be implemented, even considering the significant number of people (17 out of 41 answers—41 per cent) that answered the question without any justification. Secondly, the significant number of practical ideas given by people on how the measure should be implemented.

The second measure on the third group of analysis and last in terms of the general analysis in itself, involves the support of micro-credit initiatives to individual persons or small enterprises in order to begin or expand an economic activity. From 54 answers, 45 (83 per cent) answered positively[8] while 7 (13 per cent) answered negatively. The negative answers were based on the following arguments: there are no conditions for the economic success of these initiatives with the war (2 answers); there are too many obstacles in place such as legal and customs problems (2 answers); there are other priorities (2 answers) and there is not a sufficient flow of capital among most of the population that would allow these initiatives to be successful (1 answer). In relation to the positive answers several observations were made. Five (5) answers referred the need for this aid to include some kind of attendance (as

---

8. From the 45 answers favoring the implementation of this measure, 12 just answered 'yes' without any justification. Moreover, 7 were group answers.

some problems may occur) and supervision. Moreover, 5 alluded to the need of giving some kind of training to whom the micro-credit is attributed.

Otherwise, the credit should only be attributed to those who have some knowledge or experience in the field. Furthermore, 4 people mentioned the fact that the sums of credit have to be related with the costs in the economy. As far as the results of previous interventions in this field are concerned, 4 people said they haven't seen any results while 3 gave examples of projects which have shown positive results. In terms of the objectives of this kind of support 2 people believed it to be important to generate jobs, 2 believed it to be important to eliminate and prevent the increased poverty and 2 to increase household income, which is closely related with the previous objective. In terms of the sector of activity that this micro-credit should go for, 2 people specifically said commercial sector. They further rejected the industrial sector because they believed the conditions for its development were not in place at that moment. On the other hand, 3 people mentioned the importance of all kinds of credit, for all activity sectors. In our conclusion we would like to remark the general support to the implementation of the measure, while at the same time attention should be paid to the observations done. These observations may be at the heart of the explanation why these kinds of interventions don't often show positive results.

CHAPTER 8

CONCLUSION

Main changes in the international system underpinned the shift, in terms of aid policy, from just relief assistance towards attempts to support development in emergency situations. Namely, on the one hand, the demise of political world movements represented an alternative to the western liberal-democratic model of development and subsequent uniform way of understanding the relations among the states and the merging of security and development concerns. The increasing focus on intra-state relations made security objectives be more related to the regional implications for stability of internal matters such as poverty, population growth or migration. Insofar as approaches to development cooperation also intend to tackle these issues, there has been a merging of security and development concerns. This merging is quite relevant as it makes relief assistance no longer sufficient and makes development cooperation to be regarded as the foundation of stability.

On the other hand, the move from an international refugee regime focused almost exclusively on the obligations of receiving states, contributed to the increase in the amount of relief assistance delivered under complex political emergencies. Increasingly, no country wants to accept refugees and attempts have been prompted to prevent large scale population movements crossing international boundaries through humanitarian assistance. In addition, new operational tools, such as negotiated access, have expanded the scope of humanitarian assistance in internal wars and could be used in the same way for development interventions.

While both these facts mean that there is a wide scope for development interventions to take place under war conditions, what we have been observing is that, increasingly, in practice, development has been reduced to relief.

Dismissing the mutually exclusive nature of relief and development in emergency situations has contributed to a blurring of these categories. Rather than regarding these two as separate practices, the post Cold War paradigm holds that relief should be provided in a way to foster people-centered development, and humanitarian assistance has become the West's favored response to political crisis beyond its borders.

At a time in which development cooperation emphasizes the importance of ownership[1] and participation, we should question ourselves about what do people from war-torn countries believe in terms of promoting development in conflict situations and in terms of the increasing reduction of aid intervention to humanitarian assistance. In Angola, from the 70 interviews analyzed in this study, the majority believed in the possibility of promoting development in their country while facing a civil war. For most of them, the case seems to be of trying to do it on areas not directly affected by the war. Or else to create secured areas where that development would be pursued without alarm. A careful analysis seems to be, however, necessary in order to identify possible consequences of promoting some kind of investments in some areas while neglecting others. Especially, in countries where the concentration of the population is an important reason for its underdevelopment.

---

1. Ownership means that it will be up to developing countries themselves to engage and take development into their own hands. Development agencies will not attempt to deliver ready-made solutions. Rather they will help to create the environments in which effective ownership is possible (Pinheiro, 1998).

Moreover, even those who rejected the possibility of pursuing development in a war-torn context, consider it to be important to keep investing in development sectors while the country is in war, so that an enhanced development is possible when the war will be over. Especially education but also health are considered. (Both groups are priority areas for investing international aid at the moment.)

The education sector seems to be particularly relevant due to the realization that the massive dislocations of people to the main urban areas translate in a very significant number of children and young people staying outside school for several years. Improved education and training is considered to be an investment in people which can survive physical destruction. Moreover, there is also the belief that schools are symbolic of a return to some form of recognizable routine and are the ideal forum for reaching war affected children and adults. On the other hand, teachers are respected members of their communities and raising their aware-ness of the importance of such issues as health, girl's education and psycho-social needs is a crucial first step to long-term and culturally appropriate development in these fields.

On the other hand, our analysis also helped us clarify what is Angolan peoples opinion about the current trend of favoring humanitarian or relief assistance in relation to development cooperation. When asked about the priority field of interven-tion—social and economic development, humanitarian aid or conflict resolution—for the international aid, the majority actually answered social and economic development. For most of them, the international aid cannot promote the resolution of the conflict and the humanitarian aid, apart from generating dependency and leading to a loss of working habits, is a short-term investment which cannot promote long-term development. This belief becomes even more emphasized when they were asked the same question for the 1980s. The need for increasing investments in humanitarian aid and conflict resolution is believed to have been strongly empha-sized over the last two decades.

Conflicts, it is widely accepted, are one of the main reasons for the underdevelopment of the countries which face them.

Donor agencies and research centers, having analyzed the severe consequences of conflicts for developing countries, have been promoting several studies dealing with aid interventions in conflict situations. Varied measures have been proposed in order to prevent or diminish the impact of complex political emergencies. However, firstly, perhaps following the current trend of favoring humanitarian and rehabilitation interventions, it is difficult to find a reasonable number of development measures proposed to be implemented in war-torn countries. Secondly, from our research we concluded that, even though Angolans generally believe the measures proposed by donor agencies to be important in order to promote development in their country, they were not considered priority measures for investments to take place. Thirdly, they have specific interesting ideas of what is needed for those measures to have practical viability in their country, ideas which, according to them and in most of the cases, have not been taken into account. The point of view that people dealing with the specific realities of their countries may have important contributions to give to development agencies, is emphasized with this study. In summary, this research emphasizes how listening to the 'beneficiaries' of development cooperation views can lead to quite different results than listening to professional perspectives.

Taking into account the results of this research, there seems thus to be a need for some revision in terms of donor agencies beliefs and frameworks. The case study showed us the disagreement with the current trend of increasing relief assistance instead of development cooperation, in complex political emergencies. Furthermore, for the Angolans interviewed, the measures that have been proposed for ongoing conflicts are not a priority of investment in their country.

Reflecting their knowledge of the national reality, the measures they proposed to be implemented at the moment were greatly different from those advanced by donor agencies and research centers.

At the end of our analysis we would like to return again to the dynamics of the international system. New challenges have emerged and have to be considered also, in further studies of how to promote development in war-torn countries. The post Cold War aid paradigm seems to have, mostly, relied, so far, on the importance of the nation-state as the main intermediary for all types of development cooperation to be implemented on a specific country at a certain time. However, in view of expanded important external factors, there seems to be, increasingly, limitations to what the nation-state can achieve. New analyses suggest a more complex picture of emerging 'local' economies, disconnected from state control, run by a new type of entrepreneurs, supported by private military protection and drawing in international connections. A new political economy, 'the new medieavalism' (Cerny, 1998) seems to be imposing itself. It grows from below, and in order to survive, certain classical state functions like enforcement of property rights, protection of economic transactions, settlement of commercial disputes are reproduced in the form of Mafiatype organizations. Even NGOs and some official donors have been forced to rely on such unorthodox forms of protection and improvised logistics in order to be able to carry out their ordinary work. The conflict in certain 'countries' can be described as a clash between the new business of 'globalized' (Björn, 1999) exploitation and private protection, on the one hand, and the old nation-state project, trying to maintain the structures of a nation-state, on the other.

In this context and in the near future, private protection companies may engage themselves in more conventional development work as well, as long as there is someone to pay. What we should wonder are the consequences of this kind of dynamics. As seen previously, the main causes of conflicts seem to rely on inequality and injustice and not so much on the lack of resources *per se*. In this context, main challenges to development cooperation can be how to deal with such a multiplication of national agents and control their power in order not to exacerbate regional differences. Moreover, development cooperation will have to be able to adapt itself to the emergence of new non-state actors, at the transnational and local level, which can play a role within the aid paradigm. As Björn (1999) stated, probably, in our days of imminent globalization genuinely new structures both above and below the level of the nation-state are needed, namely 'new' transnational structures, either macro regional or micro regional or global which could provide new models of order for a new era. We would further add that the international aid community will have to be at the forefront of such evolution in order to contribute and benefit from the establishment of new models of order, improving its multidimensional effectiveness.

APPENDIX

APPENDIX 1
QUESTIONNAIRE (ANGOLA)[1]

1. Personal details
   Name:
   Age:
   Job:
       (In the case of students) Do you do something else? What do you do?
   Birth place:
       In the case of not having been born in Luanda:
       a. What are the reasons for living there at the moment?;
       b. For how long are you living in Luanda?;
       c. Where have your parents been born?.

2. How has the current situation affected you and your family?

3. Do you believe that the conflict has prevented the development of the country?

   How?

---

1. This was the entire questionnaire presented to the interviewed people. Due to the limitations of this kind of research we only analyzed the most relevant questions.

4. Do you think it's possible to pursue development in Angola in a situation of conflict?

Why?

(Yes answers) Imagine that a considerable amount of aid is deployed for Angola in order to be invested for the development of the country, even though there is a conflict ongoing. How do you think this aid should be invested?

(No answers) Imagine that a considerable amount of aid is deployed for Angola. How do you believe it should be invested, even though it is not possible to pursue development with the present conditions?

5. Now, I would like you to give me your opinion about some measures that have been proposed for war-torn societies. Namely, I would like to know whether you believe that they can and should be implemented in Angola at the moment and why.

   a. Support reform-minded elements in the society and the government/support knowledge creation in the sense of financing and evaluating innovations;
   b. Support civil society either to pressure the government to change or to take service provision into its own hands;
   c. Teach people the meaning of democratic institutions, how to defend them and how to use them as tools for absorbing conflicts;
   d. Support of institutions such as citizens' advice bureau and national and local media;
   e. Agencies should develop an understanding of the context, dynamics and assistance needs, in order to design appropriate interventions when conditions permit;
   d. Support to entities which can identify political forces and groups favoring peace and long-term reconciliation and

which can examine the benefits derived by certain groups from conflict and its perpetuation;

e.   Investments aimed at improving the capacity to cope with crisis, particularly among vulnerable groups. Example: building up emergency food and seed stocks at the community-level can contribute directly to limiting the risk of massive dislocation of people when disaster strikes, reducing the impact of humanitarian assistance;

f.   Micro-credit to individual persons or small enterprises in order to initiate or expand an economic activity.

6.   Do you know of any development project that has been or is being implemented in Angola?

(Yes answers) Which one? In your opinion, has it been achieving the proposed objectives? Why? Which organizations should implement them?

(No answers) Which organizations should implement them?

Why?

7.   In the case of Angola, do you think that presently the international aid should focus on the resolution of the conflict, on humanitarian aid or on the social and economic development?

8.   What about in the 1980s?

9.   If the conflict would stop tomorrow, which measures would be urgent?

APPENDEX 2

PERSONAL DETAILS OF THE INTERVIEWED PEOPLE

Table A-1. Number of Persons in Group Ages

Group Age	Number of Persons
<20	3
20-29	30
30-39	11
40-49	13
50-59	8
60-69	5
Total	70

Table A-2. Number of Persons for Each Profession

Profession	Number of Persons
Doctor	5
Medical laboratory technician	3
Biologist	2
Chemical technician	2
University professor	2
Professor	4
Student	19

Members of Parliament	5
Attorneys	3
Journalists	2
Oil company employee	1
Administrative secretary	1
Administrative director of a public clinic	1
Financial and administrative director of a private clinic	1
Chief of the laboratory of exploration and production of a national oil company	1
Librarian	2
Vice general director of a national N.G.O.	1
General-secretary of a national association	1
Director of studies and projections of a G.O.	1
Vice general-secretary of a G.O.	1
G.O. employee	1
Insurance broker	1
Telecommunications engineer	1
Security worker	1
Social worker	6
Priest	2
Total	70

Note: As mentioned in the methodology section, all the 70 interviews analyzed in this study were given to people having high school (40) or university (30) education. The reasons for not having included in this analysis some of the informal conversational interviews done to uneducated people were precisely the limitations of this kind of research and the fact that they were not able to answer the basic questions of the research. One example is several people interviewed in refugee camps, coming from the rural areas. Apart from the educational point of view, we also have to bear in mind that the main concern of these people is subsistence. Therefore, when they are asked about development at the moment or priorities in terms of aid investment, it is understandable that they associate development with food, shelter and water, which means humanitarian assistance.

Table A-3. Number of Persons According to the Place Where People Were Born

Provinces (Borning Place)	Number of Persons
Bié	5
Bengo	1
Benguela	1
Kuando-Kubango	3
Huíla	3
Kuanza Norte	4
Kuanza Sul	8
Luanda	27
Malange	5
Moxico	2
Uíge	5
Zaire	3
Total	67(a)

(a) We excluded the 3 Portuguese interviewed.

Table 4-A. Number of Persons That Who Born in Luanda and Outside Luanda

Provinces (Borning Place)	Number of persons
Luanda	27
Other provinces	40

Table A-5. Gender Division of the Interviewed People

Gender	Number of persons
Female	25
Male	45
Total	70

BIBLIOGRAPHY

Agerbak, L. (1991), 'Breaking the cycle of violence: doing development in situations of conflict,' *Development in Practice vol.1 no.3, p.151-158.*

Anderson, M.B. (1994), 'Understanding the disaster-development continuum: gender analysis is the essential tool,' *Focus on Gender vol.2 no.1, p.7-10.*

Buchanan-Smith, M. and Maxwell, S. (1994), 'Linking relief and development: an introduction and overview,' *Linking relief and development, IDS bulletin vol.25 no.4, p.1-16.*

Bakwesegha, C. (1998), 'Towards a Policy for Conflict Prevention in Africa: the role of the International Community' in Grandvoinnet and Schneider, *Conflict Management in Africa—a permanent challenge, p.93-98,* Development Center of the Organization for Economic Co-Operation and Development.

Campbell,W. (1994), 'Linking relief and development: an annotated bibliography,' *Development Bibliography 10,* Institute of Development Studies.

Cassen , R. (1994), *Does Aid Work?,* Oxford University Press, Oxford.

Cerny, P. G. (1998), 'Neomediavalism, Civil War and the New Security Dilemma: Globalization as Durable Disorder,' *Civil Wars, vol. 1, no.1, p.36-64.*

Colletta, N. and Nezam, T. (1998), 'The Role of Development Assistance in Conflict Prevention, Transition and Reconstruction' in Grandvoinnet and Schneider, *Conflict Management in Africa—a permanent challenge, p.99-107,* Development Center of the Organization for Economic Co-Operation and Development.

Commins, S. (1996), 'In the line of fire: development in conflict,' in: Commins, S., *Development in States of War, p.8-14,* Oxfam Publications, Oxford.

Davis, J. (1988), 'From emergency relief to long-term water development,' *Waterlines vol.6 no.4, p.29-31.*

Duffield, M. (1998), *Aid Policy and Post-Modern Conflict : a Critical Review*, The University of Birmingham, School of Public Policy, Occasional Paper 19, Birmingham.

Duffield, M. (1997), 'NGO relief in war zones: towards an analysis of the new aid paradigm,' *Third World Quarterly, vol.8, no.3, p.527-542.*

Duffield, M. (1994), 'Complex Emergencies and the crisis of Developmentalism,' *Linking Relief and Development, IDS Bulletin, vol.25, no.4, p.37-45.*

Egan, E. (1991), 'Relief and rehabilitation projects in Mozambique: institutional capacity and NGO executional strategies,' *Development in Practice vol.1 no.3, p.174-184.*

Hettne, B. (1999), 'Development and Conflict' in : *Europe and the South in the 21st Century: Challenges for Renewed Cooperation, 9th General Conference of EADI (European Association of Development Research and Training Institutes), Paris 22-25 September 1999.* Proceedings of a conference.

Joyner, A. (1996), 'Supporting education in emergencies: a case study from southern Sudan,' in: Commins, S., *Development in States of War, p.91-94,* Oxfam Publications, Oxford.

Lister, M. (1997), *The European Union and the South—relations with developing countries*, Routledge, London.

Lister, M. (1998), 'Conflict, Development and the Lomé Convention,' *European Development Policy Group—discussion paper n.12*, Development Studies Association.

Macrae & Zwi (1994), *War & Hunger—rethinking international responses to complex emergencies*, Zed Books in association with Save the Children Fund, London.

Mikkelsen, B. (1995), *Methods for Development Work and Research: a Guide for Practitioners,* Sage Publications, New Delhi.

OECD/DAC (1998), *Conflict, peace and development on the threshold of the 21st century*, Development Co-operation guidelines series, OECD Publications, Paris.

OECD (1995), *The Challenge of Development within Conflict Zones,* OECD Development Centre, OECD Publications, Paris.

Pinheiro, J. D., 'Europe's response to conflicts in Africa,' *The Courier n°168* (March-April 1998), *p.66-67.*

PNUD (1997), *Relatório do Desenvolvimento Humano—Angola 1997,* Programa das Nações Unidas para o Desenvolvimento [UNDP (1997), *Human Development Report—Angola 1997,* United Nations Development Programme].

Roche, C. (1996), 'Operationality in turbulence: the need for a change,' in: Commins, S. *Development in States of War, p.15-25,* Oxfam Publications, Oxford.

Ross, J.; Maxwell, S. and Buchanan-Smith, M. (1994), 'Linking relief and development,' *IDS Discussion Paper no.344.*

Scharf, R. (1998), 'Key findings of the OECD-DAC task force on Conflict, Peace and Development Co-operation: the imperative of conflict prevention' in Grandvoinnet and Schneider, *Conflict Management in Africa—a permanent challenge, p.109-121,* Development Centre of the Organisation for Economic Co-Operation and Development.

Seaman, J. (1994), 'Relief, rehabilitation and development: are the distinctions useful?,' *Linking Relief and Development, IDS Bulletin, vol.25, no.4, p.33-36.*

Stewart, F. (1993), 'War and underdevelopment: can economic analysis help reduce the costs,' *Journal of Internaltional Development, vol.5, no.4, p.357-380.*

UNDP (1994), *Strengthening of the coordination of humanitarian emergency assistance of the United Nations,* Report of the Secretary General, A/48/536, October 18.

World Bank Policy Research Report (1998), *Assessing Aid: what works, what doesn't and why,* Oxford University Press, Washington D.C.